Workbook for Richard C. Schwartz's
No Bad Parts

Printed Exercises for Reflection,
Processing, and Practising the Lessons

BIG ACTION BOOKS

BigActionBooks.com

Workbook for Richard C. Schwartz's *No Bad Parts* — Big Action Books

Contents

Introduction — 2
Part One: Internal Family Systems — 3
  CHAPTER ONE: WE'RE ALL MULTIPLE — 3
    EXERCISE: Getting to Know a Protector — 3
    EXERCISE: Mapping Your Parts — 6
  CHAPTER 2: WHY PARTS BLEND — 14
    EXERCISE: Unblending and Embodying — 14
  CHAPTER 3: THIS CHANGES EVERYTHING — 17
    EXERCISE: Dilemma Meditation — 17
    EXERCISE: Working with a Challenging Protector — 21
  CHAPTER 4: MORE ON SYSTEMS — 24
    EXERCISE: Daily IFS Meditation. — 24

Part Two: Self-Leadership — 26
  CHAPTER 6: HEALING AND TRANSFORMATION — 26
    EXERCISE: The Path — 26
    EXERCISE: Accessing the Self Through Unblending — 30
  CHAPTER 8: VISION AND PURPOSE — 32
    EXERCISE: Fire Drill — 32
    EXERCISE: Sad Person Meditation — 34

Part Three: Self in the Body, Self in the World — 36
  CHAPTER 9: LIFE LESSONS AND TOR-MENTORS — 36
    EXERCISE: Advanced Parts Mapping — 36
    EXERCISE: Working With Triggers — 39
  CHAPTER 10: THE LAWS OF INNER PHYSICS — 41
    EXERCISE: Advanced Protector Work — 41
  CHAPTER 11: EMBODIMENT — 44
    EXERCISE: Body Meditation — 44

Workbook for Richard C. Schwartz's *No Bad Parts* Big Action Books

Introduction

Learn to Heal Trauma, Restore Wholeness, and Embrace Every Part of Yourself.

WHY THIS WORKBOOK?

You've read Richard C. Schwartz's fabulous book about No Bad Parts. Now it's time to actually *practise* it - write; journal; put the lessons in motion.

This workbook was created as a **companion** to Richard C. Schwartz's "No Bad Parts". While reading the book, we found ourselves wishing for a place where we could write, process and practise the book's exercises in a constructive, concise way. The exercises are excellent - but there isn't much space to actually write in the book itself. Instead, we found ourselves cobbling notes together in various places - notebooks, journals, pieces of paper - all of which would eventually get lost, or at the very least, not be helpful in putting the lessons into practice. That's how this workbook was born.

HOW TO USE THIS WORKBOOK

This workbook is like a faithful friend to No Bad Parts. In it, you'll find exactly what's advertised: the exercises from the book, summarised and formatted, with space to answer.

- All exercises from No Bad Parts, extracted into one single place
- Space to write under each exercise
- Lists, ruled lines and space for you to answer, journal and reflect
- Clearly organised and well-formatted so it's easy to follow
- Space for your own freewriting and notes towards the end of the workbook.

In each section, we've extracted the main premise of the exercise, and then added space to respond and practise the lessons. This may come in the format of a table to fill in, space to free-write, or other exercise methods to provide space for reflection. You'll also notice the "Parts" and "Chapters" referenced in the book, so you can easily find the section if you need to look back on it for further context.

If you want to discover how to love every part of you by putting the lessons into practice - this workbook, as well as your own dedication, will help you do just that.

Enjoy, and thank you.
Let's dive in!

---

* Please note: This is an unofficial workbook companion for No Bad Parts to help motivated do-ers process the lessons from this fantastic book. It is not created by or associated with Richard C. Schwartz in any official way.

Part One: Internal Family Systems

CHAPTER ONE: WE'RE ALL MULTIPLE

EXERCISE: Getting to Know a Protector

Take a moment and get yourself situated. Set up as you would if you were about to meditate. If deep breaths help you, go ahead and take them.

Now, I invite you to do a quick scan of your body and mind, paying special attention to any noticeable thoughts, emotions, sensations, or impulses. It's similar to a mindfulness practice, where you simply observe what's present and create a little distance from it.

While doing that, see if any of those emotions, thoughts, sensations, or impulses are calling out to you, as if they want your attention. If you find one, try focusing exclusively on it for a minute, and observe where it seems to be located in or around your body.

As you notice it, also notice how you feel about it. Do you dislike it? Does it annoy you? Are you afraid of it? Do you want to get rid of it? Do you rely on it? Essentially, we're acknowledging that you have a connection with this thought, emotion, sensation, or impulse.

If you feel anything other than openness or curiosity toward it, ask the parts of yourself that may not like it or are afraid of it to relax a bit and give you some space to explore it without judgment.

If you can't reach that curious state, that's alright. You can spend some time talking to the parts of you that are resistant and explore their fears about engaging with the target emotion, thought, sensation, or impulse.

But if you can approach the target with mindful curiosity, then it's safe to begin interacting with it. It might feel a bit strange at first, but give it a try. By focusing on this emotion, impulse, thought, or sensation, and locating it in your body, ask if there's something it wants you to understand, and then patiently wait for an answer. Don't engage in thinking, so even your thinking parts can relax. Just wait silently, with your attention on that specific area of your body, until an answer emerges. And if nothing comes up, that's perfectly okay too.

If you receive an answer, you can follow up by asking what it's afraid would happen if it didn't manifest within you. What are its fears if it didn't act the way it does? If it responds to that question, you probably gained insight into how it's attempting to protect you.

If that's the case, try extending some appreciation to it for its efforts to keep you safe, and observe how it responds to your appreciation. Then ask this part of you what it needs from you in the future.

When you feel ready, shift your focus back to the external world and take note of your surroundings. Additionally, express gratitude to your parts for enabling this conversation and assure them that it's not their last chance to engage with you because you intend to further acquaint yourself with them.

I hope you were able to come along on that journey with me and that you gained some insights. Sometimes, the things you learn can be quite astonishing. And for me, these feelings, sensations, thoughts, urges, and other occurrences are signals from different aspects of ourselves—they're what we refer to as starting points. It's because when you focus on one of them, it's like embarking on a path that leads you to the aspect from which that thought, feeling, urge, or sensation originates. And as you become acquainted with that aspect, you'll realize that it's not just limited to that particular thought, sensation, urge, or emotion. In fact, it can offer you a range of emotions, thoughts, and insights, and it can explain its purpose and why it behaves the way it does. When you acknowledge it, it feels acknowledged by you, and you can give it the respect it deserves.

That's exactly what I began doing with my clients back in the early 1980s, and it opened up an entirely new world in the process. It reminded me of my biology class in high school when we peered through a microscope at a drop of water from a pond and were astonished to see a variety of tiny organisms like paramecia, protozoa, and amoebas scurrying around. Similarly, when we simply shift our attention inward, we discover that what we thought were random thoughts and emotions actually constitute a bustling inner community that has been interacting behind the scenes throughout our lives.

In this exercise, you might have noticed that by directing your focus to one of your aspects, you were separating yourself from it (unblending). In other words, suddenly there was an observer (you) and something being observed (the aspect). As I mentioned earlier, you'll find this type of separation in mindfulness practices, and it's an important initial step. Then you took the next step by exploring how you feel about that aspect and observing how other aspects feel about it. When you feel angry or afraid towards it, it's not the true essence of who you are, but rather other aspects that are still intertwined with your core self.

***Through this process, you turn towards what you're observing
and initiate a fresh relationship with it.***

If you managed to create space by getting those aspects to step back, it's likely that you experienced a shift towards greater mindfulness. From my perspective, accessing your core self occurred through that unblending. Simply giving other aspects room to breathe brings forth your core self, and many meditation practices aim to guide you towards that more spacious and tranquil state of mind, where a sense of calm well-being fills the void.

However, instead of merely observing what most traditions consider the ego or transient thoughts and emotions, in this process, you redirect your attention towards what you're observing and establish a new connection with it—one that involves a healthy dose of curiosity. Ideally, you can continue to deepen this relationship, and the aspects truly appreciate it when you do so. They have often been operating in isolation without any adult supervision, and most of them are quite young. When you finally turn around and give them the attention they deserve, it's like being a parent who may have been neglectful but is now becoming more nurturing and genuinely interested in their children.

Reflection:

EXERCISE: Mapping Your Parts

Okay, now I'm going to ask you to acquaint yourself with a group of interconnected elements. <u>See following pages for space to write and reflect</u>. Once again, direct your attention inward and think about another element, not the one you just dealt with, but a different one you'd like to begin with this time. You can start from any emotion, thought, belief, impulse, or sensation.

As you concentrate on this fresh element, locate it within your body or on your body. Stay focused on it until you grasp its essence well enough to depict it on the page in front of you. It doesn't have to be a masterpiece—any kind of image will do. Even a simple scribble works. Just find a way to visually represent that aspect of yourself on a blank page. Remain focused on the element until you know how to portray it, and then draw it.

Once you've captured that initial element on the page, shift your attention back to the same element in the same spot in your body. Stay focused on it until you observe a shift and another starting point—a different element—emerges. When that happens, concentrate on the second element, locate it within your body, and stay connected to it until you can also depict it on the page.

After drawing the second element, return to it once more and remain attentive until you notice another shift and a new starting point arises. Then redirect your focus to this fresh element, locate it within your body, and stay connected to it until you can represent it on the page. Once again, go back to the third element, concentrate on it in that bodily location, and simply remain present until yet another one emerges. Shift your attention to that element, locate it within your body, and stay connected to it until you can depict it.

You can repeat this process until you sense that you have mapped out a complete system within yourself. Once you feel you've accomplished that, shift your focus outward to your surroundings.

What you've likely discovered is one segment of the garlic, as we refer to it in IFS. You might be familiar with the onion analogy used in psychotherapy, where you peel off layers until you reach a core that needs healing, and then you're done. Well, in IFS, it's more like a garlic bulb. There are various cloves, each containing several interconnected elements that may be stuck in a particular past place. As you work with one clove, you'll experience relief from the burdens it holds, but you may not have addressed other cloves associated with different traumas. So, this mapping exercise aims to bring forth one subsystem within you. Feel free to continue and map out other cloves.

Now, I want you to hold your page at a distance, extending your arms with the notepad, and take a look at the four or five elements you've represented, gaining a little perspective. How do these elements relate to each other? Are there protectors among them? Do they conflict with each other? Is there any kind of alliance within them? As you begin to form some answers, make a note on your drawing to represent them.

Next, examine the elements again and explore your feelings towards each of them. Once you've done that, consider what this system needs from you. Finally, take a moment to refocus inward and express gratitude to these elements for revealing themselves to you, assuring them that this won't be the last conversation you have with them. Then shift your focus outward once again.

The following pages have space for you to write and reflect →

Workbook for Richard C. Schwartz's *No Bad Parts*

1. How I represent my part:

2. How I represent my part:

3. How I represent my part:

4. How I represent my part:

5. How I represent my part:

I suggest trying out this exercise in various situations. For instance, when faced with a significant problem in your life, take a moment to delve into it and sketch it out, and you might discover some solutions. It can help you figure out either the best course of action or the factors that are causing the difficulty. Additionally, mapping out your different aspects is a helpful technique to detach yourself from them, especially when you find yourself intertwined with multiple parts.

Notes/insights from the above:

CHAPTER 2: WHY PARTS BLEND

EXERCISE: Unblending and Embodying

This is a quick meditation that I practice daily, as do many followers of the IFS approach. I encourage you to give it a try as part of your daily routine.

Get cozy and, if it helps, take some deep breaths. Then begin by focusing on and checking in with the parts you're actively engaged with. Try to locate each of them within or around your body and show interest in how they're doing. In other words, ask if there's anything they want you to know or if they need anything—similar to how you would care for a child.

While getting acquainted with a part, at some point, help it become more familiar with who you are—the present version of yourself—because often these parts don't really know you. They have been interacting with other parts within and they often perceive you as a young child.

This might be their first encounter with the curious and caring you. Let them know your true identity, including your actual age, as they often perceive you as much younger. Inform them that they are not alone anymore and observe their reaction. If you'd like, you can even ask them how old they thought you were. You can invite them to turn around and look at you.

Once you've checked in with the parts you've started working with, you can create space and invite any other parts that require attention to come forward. Simply wait and observe what thoughts, emotions, sensations, or impulses arise. Similarly, get to know these new parts and assist them in getting to know you.

The following step is optional and may or may not occur. Revisit each part individually and invite them to relax and create space within, allowing you to be more present in your body. If a part is willing to do so, you'll notice a tangible shift in your body or mind towards a more expansive and peaceful state where that part seems to reside. If it doesn't happen, don't worry, as they may not yet know you well enough to trust that it's safe. That's perfectly fine.

If they do separate, notice the embodied and spacious sense of your being and the qualities you experience in that state. How does it feel in your body and mind now? Pay attention to the spaciousness, the sense of well-being and contentment—that feeling of being enough. Also, observe the sensation that there's nothing to do at this moment and everything is alright. Some people spontaneously feel a vibrant energy flowing through their body, tingling their fingers and toes. In IFS, we refer to this as Self energy, while others might call it chi, kundalini, or prana.

I invite you to get a physical sense of what it's like for you, your Self, to be more present in your body. Once you become somatically familiar with this state, you can recognize when you're in it and when you're not throughout your day. Any deviations from this state usually occur due to the influence of parts that have blended to some extent, leading to distracting thoughts, energy blockages, emotional constriction, or bodily tension. You can notice these activities and then reassure the parts involved that they don't have to continue behaving that way—that it's safe to separate temporarily during the meditation. Afterwards, if they wish, they can resume their attention. However, through this practice, I have discovered that parts gradually develop trust that it's safe and beneficial to allow the Self to be more present. They also trust that the Self remembers and checks in on them—that it acts as a nurturing inner parent. All of this self-leadership helps them release their caretaking roles and consider unburdening.

In the next minute or so, I invite you to shift your focus back to the external world. But before you return, express gratitude to your parts for either allowing you to be more present or for revealing their current fears and hesitations. Then, come back whenever it feels right to you.

The Four Fundamental Objectives of IFS

1. Free parts from the roles they've been compelled into, allowing them to express their true nature.

2. Restore confidence in the Self and Self-guidance.

3. Restore harmony within the internal system.

4. Enhance self-directed behavior in your interactions with the world.

This type of separating doesn't have to be confined to short sessions; it can become a lifelong practice. Throughout my day, I observe my level of embodiment, how present my true Self is. I assess the openness of my heart, whether my mind is receptive or filled with a strong agenda and pressured thoughts. I gauge the resonance of my voice when speaking and sense the flow of vibrant Self energy. I also pay attention to any physical tension in my forehead or the weight on my shoulders (where my managers reside), and so on. These are some of my personal indicators, and I encourage you to discover your own.

After years of practice, I can swiftly check these indicators and request any activated parts to relax, separate, and trust me to embody them. Since my parts now have trust in me, I often notice rapid changes in these qualities and areas within my body. However, there are a few instances where it remains challenging, indicating that I still need to address and heal certain parts that are triggered by those situations. When you can be present with your inner parts in this manner, you can lead a more authentic life in the external world.

In this meditation, I prompted you to disclose your true age to your parts. When I ask people that question (e.g., "How old do you think I am?"), approximately 70 percent of the time, the response is in single digits. Frequently, the number that comes back represents the age at which the part was compelled to abandon its inherent nature and assume its current role. Once the part took on that role, it focused solely on the external world, disregarding your growth. Consequently, many parts still believe they are protecting you as a young child. Learning your present age is often a significant revelation to these parts, and initially, they may find it hard to believe.

The objective of this updating process is for your parts to recognize that they are not the lone heroes they thought they were inside. Instead, as they begin to trust you—your true Self—as the leader within, they experience tremendous relief and can manifest their intended purpose. They may age slightly, become younger, or remain the same age, but universally, they transform into valuable roles.

Reflection:

CHAPTER 3: THIS CHANGES EVERYTHING

EXERCISE: Dilemma Meditation

Once again, I want to invite you to get cozy and take a few deep breaths. Now, think about a dilemma in your life—either one you're currently facing or one you've encountered in the past. Choose an issue that has caused a lot of internal conflict.

As you concentrate on this dilemma, observe the opposing sides and how they clash with each other. Also, pay attention to your feelings towards this battle and each side involved. Now, let's familiarize ourselves with each of those sides, one at a time.

To do this, you're going to ask one side to step aside temporarily, creating a boundary that allows you to focus on the current side you're working with. Start by getting to know the side that's not in the spotlight. Once again, take note of your emotions towards it. If any negative feelings arise, kindly ask the associated parts to let you understand it for a few minutes. We're not giving the side you're attending to more power or letting it dominate; we simply want to gain some insight. To achieve that, the side in the waiting room (or any of its allies who make themselves known) should withdraw their influence from you. You can reassure them that they'll have their turn with you later, which might help them be more patient.

If you can reach a point of curiosity about the side that's not in the waiting room, go ahead and follow that curiosity. Ask it what it wants you to know about its stance. Why does it hold such a strong position on this issue? What fears does it have about the other side taking over and winning the battle? As you listen, remember that you don't have to agree or disagree—simply convey that you respect and care about the side, that you're present with it, and that you hear it. Observe its reaction.

In the next minute or so, I'd like you to ask the side you've been conversing with to step into a separate waiting room. Then, allow the other side to emerge so you can get to know it in the same manner. Once again, strive to approach it with an open heart and an open mind as you listen to its perspective. You don't have to agree; you're simply trying to understand where it's coming from, why it's so passionate about this issue, and what it fears might happen if the opposing side were to win.

After spending some time with the second side, ask if it would be willing to have a direct conversation with the other side. Assure it that you'll act as a mediator and ensure they maintain respect towards each other. It's okay if the side isn't willing to engage in dialogue. In that case, we won't proceed to the next steps. However, if it is willing, then invite the other side to join you both and have a seat.

Now, you're going to play the role of their therapist as they engage in a conversation about this issue. Once again, it's crucial not to take sides but to help them understand each other in a different way and ensure they treat one another with respect during their discussion. Remind them that they both exist within you, so they share that commonality. Then, simply observe their reactions as they get to know each other from this new perspective. Notice what happens to the dilemma.

At some point, pause their discussion. Let them both know that you can continue meeting with them in this manner more regularly and ask if they would be willing to offer their input on future dilemmas, while trusting you to make the final decision. They would serve as advisors, rather than bearing the sole responsibility of making significant decisions like this one. Observe their reaction to this idea. As before, it can be helpful to remind them of who you are (your age, etc.) and who you are not.

In the next minute or two, express gratitude for their contributions and assure them that you'll try to reconnect. Then gradually shift your focus back to the external world.

If your components collaborated, chances are you discovered that they hardly knew each other. That's because they've held opposing roles and had exaggerated perceptions of one another. We witness a similar dynamic in international conflicts, as well as within nations, companies, families, and couples. As one side becomes more extreme, the other side feels compelled to counterbalance by becoming equally extreme in the opposite direction. This pattern occurs across all levels of human systems, particularly in the absence of effective leadership, and it holds true for our inner systems as well. Many of us have neglected our inner worlds, leaving the task of making significant decisions and resolving conflicts to our inner children while we remained occupied with external matters.

Taking a single attempt may not be sufficient to halt the ongoing battle because each part feels immense stakes, and the idea of completely relaxing is abhorrent to them. Nonetheless, they do feel a stronger connection to you and to each other. This represents a fresh kind of leadership that I encourage you to experiment with internally. In essence, it mirrors the approach I employ when working with a couple. I listen to one person, then listen to the other, thereby establishing a connection and gaining their trust. Subsequently, I bring them together, ensuring mutual respect, and encourage them to engage in this alternative mode of conversation.

Reflection:

_____

_____

_____

_____

_____

Check-In

By now, the book has guided us through four different activities aimed at helping you either familiarize yourself with your different aspects or allowing them to become acquainted with you. Perhaps it has been a smooth process and you're feeling pretty good about it. However, it wouldn't be surprising if you encountered difficulties with one or all of the exercises, or if you could only complete parts of them. A major factor influencing this is how prepared your aspects are to let you enter their world and how much trust they have in you and in each other to create space and establish boundaries. So, if they are not stepping back, it doesn't mean you're failing. It simply indicates that it will require more time to gain their trust and help them become better acquainted with you.

If you have been able to carry out the exercises, it means that, for some reason, your aspects already have a certain level of trust in you and are willing to create space. However, this isn't true for everyone. Unfortunately, some of us have had numerous negative experiences in our lives, so it might take a bit longer for our aspects to trust that engaging in this type of conversation will be beneficial.

At this stage, you might also notice peculiar occurrences during the exercises—perhaps you feel unusually tired, find yourself thinking about other tasks you need to complete, or experience headaches. None of these reactions are uncommon. When protectors are not ready, they feel the need to distract you or hinder your progress in some way. Don't resist them. My advice is to simply get to know these resistant aspects from a place of curiosity—discover what they're afraid of and respect their fears.

Notes/insights from the above:

EXERCISE: Working with a Challenging Protector

This task can be quite demanding, particularly if you're new to the field of IFS work. If that's the case for you, simply do your utmost to acquaint yourself with the aspects that aren't as prepared.

Take a moment and get cozy, preparing yourself as if you were about to engage in meditation. Think of a part of you that truly annoys or obstructs you, one that fills you with shame or that you might fear. Take a moment to identify one. What you're seeking is more of a shielding part rather than an overtly vulnerable one. Some individuals naturally gravitate toward their inner critics for this exercise, so if you're struggling to find one, that usually fits the bill.

As you concentrate on this part, observe where you sense it within or around your body, and while you focus on that location, take note of how you feel toward this part. Given what you're searching for, it's likely that you'll experience some strained emotions toward it.

Imagine placing this aspect of yourself within a confined room there. This will enable other parts of you to lower their defenses and feel somewhat safer. Make it a cozy room, but one from which it cannot escape and that you can observe through a window. Inform all the other parts that have issues with it that it will remain contained for the duration of the exercise. Ask them to relax a little so that you can reach a point of curiosity toward the one in the room—see if they're willing to cooperate.

If they're unwilling to separate, once again, that's alright. You can spend the remainder of the time simply getting to know them and their fears regarding this other part or the problems they have with it. If you manage to reach a state of curiosity or any form of openness toward the part in the room, let it know and discover what it wants you to understand while it remains contained. Try communicating with it through the window. What does it want you to know about itself? What does it fear would happen if it were to step out of its role?

If it provides an answer to that question, try expressing some gratitude to it for at least attempting to protect you and determine its perception of your age. If it believes you're a different age than you actually are, go ahead and update its understanding. Observe its reaction.

Now, ask this part a variation of the following question: "If you could change or resolve what you're safeguarding so that it no longer posed a significant issue, and you were released from the responsibility of protection, what would you like to do instead?" In other words, if the part were completely liberated from its role, what else would it choose to engage in? After it responds to that question, inquire about what it requires from you in the future.

Then, before we conclude, check in with your other parts. Observe how they react as they witness the conversation you had with the protective part.

When it feels appropriate, I encourage you to conclude your time there, expressing gratitude to your parts for anything they allowed to transpire, and letting them know that this won't be your last visit. If it helps, take deep breaths again, and shift your focus back to the outside.

A few years back, I received an invitation to speak briefly at the Mind & Life Europe conference, where the Dalai Lama was present. During our conversation, I discussed the topics I've been covering here and posed a question to him. I asked, "Your Holiness, you encourage us to show compassion to our enemies or at least view them with compassion. What if we extended that compassion to our inner enemies as well?" This exercise aims to explore our inner adversaries. Initially, it may be challenging to feel compassion towards them, but it's important to approach them with an open mind and genuinely try to understand them.

I'm not sure if you've experienced this, but if you persist and ask nonthreatening questions, these inner enemies will unveil their hidden stories, revealing how they ended up in their roles and what they are protecting. In many cases, they were actually heroes. As Henry Wadsworth Longfellow once wrote, "If we could glimpse the secret history of our enemies, we would discover enough sorrow and suffering in each person's life to disarm all hostility."

These inner enemies are essentially good parts compelled to play unwanted roles.

When we approach our inner enemies and listen to their secret histories, it naturally diminishes the hostility in other parts of ourselves that resisted them. This is highly beneficial for our inner enemies. They are all good parts trapped in unwanted roles that they long to abandon, but they hesitate because they don't perceive it as safe. One reason for their lack of trust is their uncertainty in your leadership. By engaging with them in this manner, you contribute to building that trust.

One more thing: As you engage in this practice, you may notice shifts occurring both internally and externally. Embracing this new perspective makes it difficult to view people in the same light, leading to a change in how you relate to them. While some individuals may struggle with these transformations in you, others will undoubtedly welcome them.

Reflection:

CHAPTER 4: MORE ON SYSTEMS

EXERCISE: Daily IFS Meditation.

Here's a meditation that I and other practitioners of Internal Family Systems (IFS) use to encourage this change in perspective within ourselves. I recommend practicing a variation of it daily on your own.

Begin by taking a moment to find your comfort. If it helps, you can take a few deep breaths to center yourself. If you've already tried the exercises mentioned earlier, you're likely familiar with some of your inner parts. I invite you to focus on those parts that you're becoming acquainted with first. The aim is to check in on them, see how they're doing now, and if there's anything they require or want you to know. This helps establish an ongoing connection with your parts, making them feel more connected to you and less alone.

At some point, remind them that you're there for them and that you genuinely care. Share a bit more about yourself because, even as you work with your parts, they often forget these things until they've been relieved of their burdens. It's always good to remind them that they are no longer alone, and you are no longer a young child incapable of taking care of them in the way they need.

The goal is to treat your parts as seriously as you would treat your own children, if you have any. The good news is that your parts don't require nearly as much attention or nurturing as actual children do—they mainly need to be aware of the connection you're building and be reminded of it.

Then, at a certain point, you can expand your focus and invite any other parts that need attention to come forward. Different parts may surface on different days. Take the time to get to know them and understand what they need from you. Let them also know who you are and that they are no longer alone.

Now, here's an optional element for each meditation: If you wish, you can revisit each of these parts and invite them to relax in an open, spacious environment for a few minutes. Ask them to trust that it's safe to allow you to be more present in your body. Their energy can sometimes hinder your embodiment when they are triggered. If they are willing to let you in further, you'll notice a shift each time they relax—you'll experience more internal space in your mind and body. Reassure them that it's only for a few minutes, an experiment to see what happens if they allow you to be more present. They don't have to if they don't want to; in that case, continue getting to know them. However, if they are willing, observe the qualities of this increased spaciousness and embodiment. Notice how it feels to be more grounded in your body with ample space.

You may observe changes in your breathing or your ability to be fully present. Your muscles might relax, and a sense of well-being may emerge, as if everything is alright. As mentioned earlier, you may also sense a kind of energy flowing through your body, causing slight trembling or tingling in your extremities. Personally, I'm attuned to sounds, so I notice changes in my voice tone when I'm in this state. I also appreciate the tranquility that accompanies the absence of a pressing agenda.

If your parts struggle to relax, it simply means they need more attention at some point. Let them know you understand, and there's no pressure for them to do anything. When it feels appropriate, you can gradually shift your focus back to the present moment, thank your parts for the insights they provided, and assure them that you'll continue this practice in the future. Take a few deep breaths if it helps you return to the present state.

As I go about my day, I often take a moment to observe how frequently I find myself in this state. When I'm not, it indicates that some aspect has taken control or is at least more dominant, and I can swiftly locate that part and reassure it that it can trust me, that it can relax a bit and create more space. It has taken time, but now, in nearly every situation, my parts readily respond and I can sense the renewed energy and expansiveness, allowing me to connect with people from that state.

This has become a daily routine. Besides recognizing the parts and helping them trust in opening up space, it is usually necessary to actively engage with them and facilitate healing because as long as your system remains vulnerable, it will be difficult for them to place trust in you. Thus, in conjunction with this meditation, both I and other IFS practitioners actively conduct sessions to alleviate burdens carried by these parts.

Reflection:

_____

_____

_____

_____

_____

Part Two: Self-Leadership

CHAPTER 6: HEALING AND TRANSFORMATION

EXERCISE: The Path

In this section of the book, where we explore Self-leadership, I want to share a practice with you to help you connect with your inner Self and its energy.

Once again, find a comfortable position and take deep breaths if it helps. Now, imagine yourself standing at the beginning of a path. It could be a familiar path you've traveled before or a completely new one. Gather your inner parts at the starting point and kindly ask them if they would be willing to wait there for a while, allowing you to embark on this brief solo journey.

Observe their reactions to this suggestion. See if the fearful parts can find comfort from the more courageous ones. Let them all know that it won't take long and that it will benefit everyone involved, but reassure them that they don't have to agree if they're not ready. It's natural for them to feel differently on different days. If they prefer not to proceed, spend some time getting to know them better and understanding their fears about allowing you to undertake this journey.

However, if they are open to the idea, go ahead and start walking along the path, reminding them that you'll return shortly. Along the way, I'll pause and ask you to notice certain things, but for now, simply begin your journey.

Now, I invite you to pay attention to what unfolds as you continue on this path. Specifically, observe any thoughts that arise, as thoughts indicate the presence of accompanying parts. If you notice such parts, ask them if they would be willing to separate and rejoin the others. If they hesitate, explore the source of their fear.

Additionally, scan your body for any sensations that feel unfamiliar or different from your usual Self. If you come across any, they are likely parts as well. Request those parts to return to the starting point. As they comply, you will gradually feel a shift towards pure awareness, with fewer thoughts occupying your mind. If some parts are unwilling to leave, that's perfectly fine—use this time to understand their fears better.

If, at any moment, you find yourself observing yourself on this journey, it means that a part is attempting to take over.

Take a moment to identify that part and kindly request it to return to the starting point. As you continue on the path, try to experience your surroundings directly, without watching yourself from a distance.

If your parts trust you enough to allow this process, you should now begin to experience some of the qualities we discussed earlier—clarity, a quiet mind, spaciousness, being present in the moment, a sense of well-being, connection, embodiment, confidence, and more. You might also feel a subtle, vibrating energy flowing through your body. We call this Self energy. If you sense this energy, invite it to circulate throughout your entire being.

If you encounter any areas where the energy seems blocked, there may be a part hindering its flow for some reason. You can inquire if that part would be willing to return to the starting point as well. If you don't experience these qualities, it means that some parts are still accompanying you. Take a moment to scan your body and mind, locating those parts, and kindly ask them to return to the base.

At some point, pause and fully immerse yourself in this experience. Take note of what it feels like to have such a strong connection with your inner Self. Observe the various ways you can sense it and where it manifests in your body. Remember these signs; they indicate your embodiment. As you go about your day, you can gauge how present you are, how much influence your parts have.

Personally, I often check the openness of my heart, whether my mind is excessively busy, or if I feel tension in my shoulders and forehead, which are areas where my controlling parts tend to reside. When I notice any of these parts taking charge, I simply ask them to relax and, in a way, return to the starting point and observe as I handle the situation. I reassure them by saying, "Just trust me." Some parts may offer guidance before stepping back, and that's perfectly fine.

If, by this point, you're experiencing a significant amount of Self energy and embodiment, you can choose to invite messages from the universe. It's possible that nothing will come, and that's perfectly okay. However, sometimes people receive clear guidance during moments like this.

Now, let's make our way back to the starting point at a pace that feels right to you. When you reunite with your parts, observe their reactions to your return and express gratitude for the risks they took in allowing you to undertake this journey. Ask them about their experience and if they would be open to trying it again sometime. Once again, remind them that you are there to support them and earn their trust. If any parts haven't trusted you for any reason, assure them that you are open to understanding and healing those concerns. If you still feel the tingling Self energy, you can direct it towards your parts.

It's remarkably healing and can be extended to both your internal parts and other people. I extend it to my clients during our sessions. Observe how your parts respond to receiving the Self energy you have to offer.

When you feel complete with this process, once again express your gratitude to your parts for participating in this exercise and gradually shift your focus back to the external world. However, try to retain some of this Self state even as you open your eyes and return to your surroundings.

Some folks don't make much progress along the path. Due to various reasons, their components prevent it. Nevertheless, it's valuable to understand why. Inquire about their lack of trust and address their fears.

However, if components are willing to wait at the starting point and let you venture down the path alone, it's a common experience for people to encounter what I've described. A sense of self-energy emerges naturally once your components allow you to fully embody yourself, and you can direct that energy towards yourself or others as wanted. Personally, I don't extend it to individuals unless I'm certain it's welcomed, but I do encourage you to extend it to components regardless of their consent, as they simply seem to adore it.

When I invite you to seek any messages, it's not unusual for nothing to occur. Nonetheless, there are instances where people receive clear guidance about their lives or how to work with their components. Other times, it's simply a warm and comforting feeling that they're not alone. If you do receive information at this stage, share it with your components.

As for the source of this information, I don't take a stance on the matter. Whether it's your intuition, a wise aspect of yourself, a spirit guide, or anything else—I'll let you discover that for yourself. I'll just say that based on empirical observation, when individuals are fully in tune with themselves and seek a message, something useful often emerges.

Another significant aspect of this exercise is that it often compels you to notice components that would otherwise go unnoticed. We all have managers who resemble the Self or are somewhat like the Self. We don't typically recognize them because they're so blended in and involved in most of our interactions with the world. They often believe they are us, and we tend to believe that too. However, they're simply highly convincing types of protectors. They make us appear kind, polite, and caring, for instance, but only to persuade others to like us and view us favorably. Additionally, they often bear the responsibility of keeping certain disapproved parts in exile.

Unlike the Self, these Self-like managers have protective agendas and aren't completely authentic when expressing care, gratitude, or respect. Some people derogatorily refer to them as the ego, but they deserve our love rather than our scorn. Similar to any other protector, we need to alleviate them of their overwhelming burdens of responsibility.

Reflection:

EXERCISE: Accessing the Self Through Unblending

Similar to the exercise you just completed, this activity will assist you in exploring how the Self functions within you. As you usually do before starting these exercises, take a moment to find your comfort and take deep breaths if it helps. Once again, we'll check in with the parts of you that you're actively getting to know and simply observe how they're doing today. Remind them that you're present with them, ready to provide assistance and care. You can also broaden your awareness to include other parts that you may not be familiar with—acknowledge their presence, express your care for them, and let them know that you're committed to getting to know them better.

When you feel that your parts have been acknowledged by you, request them to relax and create space within your mind and body. Reassure them that this will only be temporary and that the purpose of this exercise is to uncover more about your true self.

If they are willing, you'll experience a similar expanded and spacious awareness as you did in the previous exercise. This time, try to see if they would allow you to maintain this state of Self-leadership even when you open your eyes. So if your eyes have been closed until now, experiment with opening them and see if you can still sense the spaciousness. It's possible that some parts might immediately become vigilant and protective when you open your eyes.

The act of opening your eyes in that state is a step towards experiencing a sense of being Self-led and fully present in your everyday life. By "practice," I don't mean that Self-leadership is something you have to gradually develop like a muscle. In this exercise, we are instead helping your parts build trust, enabling them to allow you to embody and lead, and assuring them that it is safe. The more they give it a try and witness that nothing dreadful occurs, the more willing they will be to continue exploring it. Over time, you can increasingly experience this alternative way of being and extend it to your daily life.

Once you finish this activity, remember to express gratitude to your parts for their contributions and shift your focus back to the external world. Also, observe how much you can maintain this sense of Self as you return to your daily activities.

Reflection:

CHAPTER 8: VISION AND PURPOSE

EXERCISE: Fire Drill

So now I'd like to suggest an activity that can help you get a taste of the Self-leadership I've been discussing. Let's begin by thinking of someone in your life (past or present) who really gets under your skin. Perhaps they make you feel angry or sad, or maybe there's a person you've distanced yourself from emotionally.

Imagine this person being in a room, isolated and unable to leave at the moment. Now, picture yourself looking at them through a window. As you observe them from outside the room, imagine them saying or doing the things that bother you, and pay attention to how your body and mind react when your protective instincts kick in. Notice the impact on your muscles, your heart, and any impulses you experience. Also, pay attention to your breathing. The goal is to simply observe how your body and mind respond to this protective part.

Now, take another look at the person, but this time, try to see them through the lens of your protector. Reassure your protector that you won't enter the room, allowing it to relax a bit. See if it's willing to separate its energy from you, knowing that you won't put yourself at risk. As it withdraws its energy, you'll likely feel a noticeable shift in your body and mind.

How do your muscles feel now? What about your heart and breathing? Take note of what's happening in your mind as well. Then, look at the person in the room again and see if they appear any different. How does their image change?

Now, shift your focus back to the protector that arises when you think about this person. Try to cultivate curiosity towards it now that it's a bit more separate from you. If possible, ask the protector why it feels the need to be so strong when dealing with this person. What is it afraid would happen if it didn't intervene on your behalf?

In answering this question, the protector might reveal vulnerable parts that it's safeguarding. If that's the case, show appreciation for its efforts in protecting those aspects of yourself. Observe how it reacts to your gratitude. Ask the protector if it would still need to be so involved in safeguarding those parts if you could heal them, making them less vulnerable to this person. What alternative roles might it take on within you?

Remember, we won't actually enter the room with the triggering person during this exercise. However, try to get a sense of what it would be like if you did. Imagine stepping into that room while being more Self-led. How do you think it would unfold? How would your interactions with this person change?

If you find it challenging to envision this scenario, it could be because your protector doesn't fully trust that it's safe for you to do so. If you do have a sense of how different the experience would be, communicate that to your protector and inquire about what it would take for that part to trust you as the leader when facing individuals who trigger you. And if your protector still hesitates to trust you, ask for more insight into its concerns.

When you feel ready, express gratitude to this part for its contributions. Acknowledge whatever it allowed you to do or understand. Finally, shift your focus outward again and take deep breaths if it helps you transition.

During this activity, if your guardian moved aside, you probably experienced a significant change. While conversing with your guardian, you likely gained insights into the parts it safeguards and their vulnerability. Since those vulnerable parts were not healed through the exercise, it's probable that the guardian will withhold trust until they are healed. However, it's still intriguing to understand the reasons behind its lack of trust in your ability to handle such situations.

You might have also observed that when the guardian stepped back, your body sensed a difference, and the person in the room appeared altered. Perhaps they didn't appear as threatening, and you could perceive some of the pain that drove them to engage in harmful actions.

Reflection:

_____

_____

_____

_____

_____

EXERCISE: Sad Person Meditation

Let's try out a similar activity. Instead of thinking about someone who triggers you, imagine a different person who was extremely upset—like really sad and hurt, maybe even crying. Take a moment to recall this person and, just like before, picture them inside a small room. Observe them through the window as they express their pain and sadness.

While you watch, pay attention to how your body and mind respond. Take note of the thoughts that arise about this person (even if they're not the most positive), and observe the various aspects of yourself that react to them. Notice how these parts of you impact your body—do they affect your heartbeat, breathing, muscles, or impulses? Some parts might make it challenging to watch the person in the room. They could make you feel powerless, inclined to withdraw or run away, keep your emotions guarded, or exhibit other protective behaviors.

Choose one of these parts and take some time to understand it better. Assure it that at this moment, there's no need to take action for this person, and they will remain in the room. Encourage the part to relax a little and detach, if possible. If it does, observe the noticeable shift and then look at the person in the room through this new perspective. Envision how you would like to be with this person if your parts didn't interfere.

Just like before, shift your attention back to the protective part and inquire about its fears regarding what would happen if it didn't act this way within you. Why does it lack trust in your ability to stay present with the person? Once you feel that this part of the exercise is complete, express gratitude to this protector for its efforts and gradually shift your focus back to the external world.

Reflection:

_____

_____

_____

_____

_____

These two activities demonstrate how we encourage Self leadership. I employ a method called constraint-releasing to access Self. Instead of attempting to imbue positive qualities through a process some refer to as resourcing, I invite you to identify the aspects that hinder your connection to Self. Then, you can familiarize yourself with those parts and assist them in developing trust in your ability (your Self) to handle challenging individuals.

In a complete IFS session, I would ask for your permission to explore the parts protected by those guardians and facilitate their healing. By doing so, your guardians become more inclined to trust your leadership.

Frequently, your guardians doubt your capacity to fulfill the demanding task of protection because they perceive the Self as fragile, capable only of kindness and empathy. Based on my experience, the Self possesses proficiency in all the C-words associated with treating others well, including lucidity, assurance, and bravery. Consequently, when you view the actions of others that cause harm to your parts through the clear perspective of your Self, there is no need to demonize them. This clarity empowers you to recognize that their behavior arises from their own pain, while also enabling you to discern the harm inflicted upon your parts without confusion. Consequently, you possess the confidence and courage to establish effective boundaries with them, even if it requires assertiveness.

Assisting your parts in developing trust in your ability to handle people and establish protective boundaries is crucial. In fact, if they trust you to do so, the impact will be more influential and successful. Ideally, this is fostered in the realm of martial arts—protection from a position of detachment yet strength. As you encounter triggering situations, it becomes intriguing to observe the bodily and mental responses. You will start to notice trails that lead you to explore the parts that feel compelled to protect. If you have access to a therapist or a proficient IFS practitioner, you can undergo the healing steps with their support. Through this process, your parts will gradually increase their trust in you and become less susceptible to triggering in the future.

Notes/insights from the above:

Part Three: Self in the Body, Self in the World

CHAPTER 9: LIFE LESSONS AND TOR-MENTORS

EXERCISE: Advanced Parts Mapping

You've already completed a similar exercise (Mapping Your Parts) earlier in this book. Now, we'll delve into the advanced version, where you'll use tor-mentors to identify and engage with the specific part that was activated by a person or event, like a clove of garlic.

Let me share a personal example: I was diligently working on a presentation this morning when I suddenly realized that I had forgotten to join an important call involving my five brothers. We needed to discuss some business matters, and there was even a lawyer on the call. Unfortunately, I was the only brother who missed it. As the eldest among the six of us, I didn't fit the conventional mold of an older sibling, being the least responsible one. Growing up, my father constantly reminded me of that. I have a critical part that can mimic my father's voice quite well whenever I make a mistake, and I immediately noticed it kicking in today. Although it has changed over the years, it still has some influence whenever I make a significant error. Consequently, an exile is triggered, and I experience a rush of shame coursing through my body.

I felt deeply disappointed when this occurred. Despite the personal growth I've undergone, I thought I had moved past this level of internal reactivity. However, since I'm committed to using such incidents as opportunities for growth, I promptly called the person with whom I exchange sessions and used the entire incident as the focus for further healing work.

I share this story to encourage you to consider a situation that you'd like to explore further and understand the different parts involved. Before you begin, though, I want to mention that you'll be learning a bit about the protectors of your exiles. Please note that you won't directly approach the exile itself, but for some individuals, simply learning about their exiles can be triggering. If at any point during the exercise it feels overwhelming, take a pause, step out of the practice, and check in with yourself. Remind your parts that you're present. If that helps, resume the exercise; if not, you can skip this particular one.

Recall a moment when you were significantly triggered by something. As you think about that situation, observe the parts that were activated, and then select one protector from that group to focus on. Direct your attention solely towards that protector, locating it within or around your body, and take note of your feelings towards it. If you experience any intense emotions, such as fear, towards that part, remember that it's just another aspect of yourself. In that case, briefly shift your focus to that particular part.

Like we did before in the dilemma exercise, take note of those two individuals—the original guardian and the one with the attitude—and observe how they clash within you. You can also pay attention to any other protectors that join in, aligning with one side or perhaps taking a different stance altogether.

For now, we aren't engaging with these parts directly; we're simply gaining an understanding of this network that emerges when triggered in your life. We're getting acquainted with the protectors that have stepped forward thus far. At some point, as you witness this interplay among your protectors, try to open your mind further to them so you can learn about their nature. If you can't quite reach that point, that's alright—just focus on observing. However, if you do find yourself intrigued by all this activity, go ahead and inquire about the vulnerability each protector is safeguarding. What do they fear would happen if they didn't take their current position?

By asking this question to your protectors, you'll begin to uncover the exiles that fuel these intense reactions. Without directly delving into those exiles, see if you can get a sense of them. Can you make an educated guess about their characteristics? Can you become more aware of their vulnerabilities?

As you discover more about what your protectors are trying to protect, it may help you develop a greater sense of empathy towards them. You gain a deeper understanding of what they're grappling with and the high stakes involved. Often, these protectors resemble parents with an extremely vulnerable child. They argue and become polarized about the best way to shield that child, given the significant consequences if the child were harmed. The distinction here is that these protectors aren't mature enough to be parents—usually, they are young themselves, overwhelmed, and striving to do their utmost.

> ***The events occurring in that inner realm have significant consequences for what unfolds in the external realm.***

Make sure to convey your understanding of everything. Inform them that you'll continue collaborating. And give a heads up to those who are confined — you can't meet them right now, but you plan to assist them later. Remember, what occurs in that inner realm greatly affects the outer realm.

Now shift your focus outward and redirect your attention to the outside world. You're exiting your internal realm, but you're not neglecting it.

Sometimes this exercise can be a tad challenging, particularly as you delve into the realm of exiles. It can be unsettling to acknowledge their presence, and occasionally—even if I advised against it—you catch glimpses of their anguish, fear, or shame, along with the beliefs they carry. This can trouble the protectors who have been diligently containing them all this time. It's not uncommon to feel somewhat overwhelmed, and I understand that it can be tough. Often, when we even lightly touch an exile, there's a strong reaction from protective parts that are afraid or may want to criticize you now. However, if you maintain the perspective that their reactions stem from fear, you can offer reassurance and help them remember your true essence. Perhaps that can assist you in staying grounded.

You possess bravery, confidence, clarity, a sense of connection, and groundedness. If you experience anything that suggests otherwise, just remember that those messages originate from parts that are unfamiliar with who you truly are. Keep in mind that they often perceive you as much younger than you actually are. It's beneficial not to completely merge with them or immerse yourself in their world. Instead, reassure them, create some distance, and help them trust that these explorations are challenging but manageable because you are no longer a little child—you are here to assist them.

Reflection:

EXERCISE: Working With Triggers

If a few of your components were activated during the previous exercise, here's a practical exercise to assist you with that.

Observe the sensations in your body and thoughts after delving into your inner world for a few minutes. If any of your components were triggered, instead of merging with them, simply notice their presence. While doing so, kindly request them to separate from you just a bit so that you can be present with them without fully identifying as them. If possible, approach their triggers with curiosity from this slightly detached state. Ask yourself why these triggers were challenging for them. What message do they want to convey? While you remain alongside them without fully immersing in their experience, try to reassure them that you are still present. Remind them that you possess maturity and can offer assistance. Acknowledge that this work is difficult and may be intimidating for some of your components, but assure them that you are there with them.

As you engage with these components in a compassionate manner, gently remind them that you have been caring for both them and yourself for a considerable period. You possess wisdom on how to improve well-being for everyone involved, and you intend to act upon that wisdom. When the timing feels appropriate, engage in activities that help you shift your focus back to the external world.

I hope you managed to complete these exercises and gained some insights into your guardians and their protective roles. When I work with couples and they find themselves in conflict, I suggest that each of them take a break, turn their attention inward, and engage in similar practices. My wife and I do the same whenever we have a disagreement. We both pause, give ourselves some time alone, focus internally, identify the voices speaking within us, listen to them, acknowledge what they're safeguarding, and then reconnect with each other and express the perspectives of those voices from a more open-hearted standpoint. When we are able to do this, it makes a significant difference. We don't always achieve complete success, but generally, the outcome is much better than when I allow my protective instincts to dominate the conversation.

Many interactions end up becoming battles between protectors. We witness this in various contexts such as corporations, families, and politics. In countries like the US, divisions escalate due to the overpowering influence of different factions on each side. When one faction becomes extreme, it triggers an equally extreme response from the protector of the opposing party, or even a more extreme reaction, and this pattern continues to escalate over time.

This is especially true when both sides lack trust in the overall leadership and have numerous suppressed voices. This dynamic applies to all levels of human systems.

Many interactions turn into protector battles.

I conduct training sessions for mediators, conflict resolution experts, and social activists, all of whom find this process beneficial. Using language like "A part of me was deeply affected by your recent comment, and beneath that part, there was another part that felt hurt" conveys a significantly different message compared to saying, "I really didn't like what you just said." Moreover, it leads to different and more predictable outcomes. Being guided by our authentic selves and representing the various parts within us is not limited to exploring our inner world. It also influences how we navigate the external world and interact with other individuals and their own inner parts.

Reflection:

CHAPTER 10: THE LAWS OF INNER PHYSICS

EXERCISE: Advanced Protector Work

We embrace the motto of welcoming all parts. However, there are certain parts that we feel more uneasy or embarrassed about.

Similar to previous exercises, take a moment to relax and find your comfort zone. If it helps, you can take deep breaths or prepare yourself as if you were about to meditate. Begin by checking in with the parts you have previously worked on. See how they are doing and remind them that you are there for them and genuinely care.

I believe that growing up in the United States or other countries with a lengthy history of racism inevitably leaves a mark (although I have noticed that people from some nations don't carry it). Regardless of your race or the extent of your anti-racism efforts, it's probable that a part of you still carries that weight. I adore a story shared by Desmond Tutu about boarding a plane and feeling proud to see two black pilots. However, during the flight, he caught himself worrying about the absence of a white pilot!

This anecdote illustrates that racism resides within all of us. By shaming and banishing that part, we only perpetuate implicit racism, leading to more blind spots and sustaining the overarching system of racism.

Therefore, I invite you to examine that specific aspect—the racist part. The part that harbors white supremacist beliefs and occasionally utters hurtful thoughts in your mind. I have conducted this practice with numerous individuals, and even those who initially deny any awareness of their own racism eventually uncover it if they exercise patience.

I am not urging you to embrace that racist part. Instead, I want you to take note of how you feel towards it. And when another part speaks up—especially one that prompts you to feel ashamed or fearful of your racist part—simply inform that protector that approaching the racist part will actually aid in its transformation. Let them know that the approach of exile they adopt is ineffective.

Right now, it might be sufficient to acknowledge the presence of the racist aspect and commit to engaging in further collaboration with someone who can assist you.

Here are some helpful reminders from the perspective of Internal Family Systems (IFS):

- That inner racist represents just one part of you. Most of your being is not characterized by that mindset.
- It's not an insurmountable bundle of racism. Similar to your other protectors, this part can be relieved and transformed as well.
- There's no need to feel ashamed of harboring this part. Racism is a deeply ingrained burden within our culture.
- If you're similar to me and many individuals I've worked with, this burden of cultural legacy permeates multiple aspects. Therefore, don't be disheartened if it doesn't completely vanish once you alleviate one of them.

Eventually, you may discover that this racist part serves as a protector, and it's necessary to heal the suppressed aspect it safeguards before it can unburden itself. Alternatively, the part may solely carry the burden of racism's cultural legacy, and it will readily unload it once you communicate that it's possible.

As always, when you feel you've reached a suitable point, express gratitude to your parts for their contributions and return to the external world. Employ any means necessary to transition out of this work and prioritize self-care.

Growing up with parents involved in the civil rights movement, I've always considered myself an active supporter of progressive causes. However, when I decided to directly address issues of racism, I was shocked to discover a prejudiced aspect within me. I'm not sure why, but it has been one of the most challenging parts for me to confront and let go of. Occasionally, I still experience its influence and have to gently challenge its beliefs and impulses. This aspect feels young and fearful. I believe many people can relate to this, and my aim is to promote a less polarized conversation about racism, encouraging greater openness and acknowledgment of our internal struggles.

Instead of trying to rid yourself of your racist tendencies, it's more beneficial to simply acknowledge their existence. When you encounter such a tendency, you can compassionately remind it that you're aware of its presence, but its thoughts and beliefs are misguided. The problem arises when you engage in a battle against your inner racism. As I've mentioned before, fighting against a part usually only strengthens it. By suppressing and denying its existence, you may temporarily feel better about yourself, but it becomes much harder to address and counteract its potential harm.

I encourage you to apply a similar approach when dealing with other aspects that bring you shame or fear—perhaps the one that gives rise to embarrassing sexual fantasies, or the one that admires Donald Trump, or the part that secretly revels in your friends' failures, or the part that believes in male superiority over women. We all have aspects we prefer not to admit, even to ourselves. Generally, these aspects are like misguided inner children. Just as we would guide and love external children, we should extend the same care and understanding to these aspects, rather than treating them with scorn, shame, or abandonment.

Reflection:

CHAPTER 11: EMBODIMENT

EXERCISE: Body Meditation

Here's the final exercise I'd like to suggest, which is connected to the thoughts about your body we've been discussing. While reading, you may have considered your relationship with your body and any symptoms you've experienced. I want to emphasize that I don't assume your symptoms or tensions are necessarily caused by specific factors. Moreover, I don't want to imply that you're intentionally causing these issues. That's not the message here. It's not you who wants to have a symptom; it's simply a small part within you. Often, this part is unaware of the overall impact it has on your body and your loved ones. Once you genuinely listen to that part, it will stop causing harm.

Now, I invite you to direct your attention to your body. If you have a medical condition, you can focus on how it manifests. If not, just find a place in your body that doesn't feel quite like you—any area with tension, pressure, congestion, discomfort, or fatigue. We're searching for a starting point—an aspect to concentrate on as we embark on this exploration. Take a moment to locate such a spot.

Once you've identified it, bring your attention to that area and observe how you feel about it. You might feel frustrated, defeated, or wish to eliminate it, and those reactions are understandable. However, for our purposes, we'll kindly ask those reactions to step back momentarily, allowing you to simply acquaint yourself with that sensation. If you can shift to a curious mindset, inquire what it wants you to understand.

Take a moment and wait for a response. Let go of any speculative thoughts and if no answer arises, that's okay. It could be purely a physical matter unrelated to your internal aspects. However, if you do receive a response, treat the sensation as if it were a part of you and continue asking it questions, similar to how we address different aspects within ourselves. For example, you can ask, "What do you fear would happen if you didn't affect my body in this way?"

If it answers that question, you'll gain insight into how it tries to protect you, and you can express gratitude towards it. However, it's possible that it isn't a protector but simply attempting to communicate a message to you. In that case, another helpful question would be, "Why do you feel the need to use my body? Why don't you feel comfortable communicating with me directly?" Lastly, you can ask something like, "What do you require from me to avoid affecting my body in this manner?"

Once again, when you feel ready, you can thank the part for any information it shared (if applicable) and gradually shift your focus outward, taking deep breaths if it helps.

Here's a method to explore a fresh connection with your body. Whenever you experience a feeling or sign, give it your focus. What is it attempting to communicate with you?

Reflection:

You made it to the end!

Thank you.

Thank you so much for picking up the Workbook for Richard C. Schwartz's *No Bad Parts*. We really hope you enjoyed it, and that it helped you practise the lessons in everyday life.

If you'd like to give feedback on the book, or to find more workbooks for other self-development books, join us at BigActionBooks.com.

Thanks again,
The Big Action Books team

BIG ACTION BOOKS

BigActionBooks.com

Notes

Notes

Notes

Notes

Notes

Notes

Notes

Notes

Notes

Workbook for Richard C. Schwartz's *No Bad Parts*

Notes

Notes

Notes

Notes

Made in the USA
Las Vegas, NV
21 November 2023